What Leaders and Parents Think of Promoting Student Success

My dad, Zig Ziglar, often said, "We don't always need to be told, but we often need to be reminded." *Promoting Student Success* is a great reminder of what is necessary for the growth and development of successful students to successful adults.

– Tom Ziglar, proud son of Zig Ziglar, CEO, Ziglar, Inc.

This inspiring book shows you how to help your children connect to their passions, realise their dreams, and create a life of responsibility and joy.

– Marshall Goldsmith, author of the *New York Times* and *Wall Street Journal* #1 best seller, *Trigger*

No instruction manual comes with children. Raising them requires care. In *Promoting Student Success*, Kelly Benedict provides that instruction manual for parents, giving much needed and practical advice on what parents should do and how they should do it.

– William J. Rothwell PhD, Bestselling Author and Professor Pennsylvania State University

Promoting Student Success is an excellent guide for parents who are navigating the complexities of helping their children achieve their aspirations. Every parent should read it and implement the ideas.

– Ed Cohen, Executive Vice President, Nelson Cohen Consulting

Fast paced book, with real life examples and thought provoking messages. A must read for any new parents, existing parents, or anybody thinking about having children. Kelly has knocked it out of the park, and parents will be using this material for years to come.

– Bill Dow, author of *The Project Management Communication Bible*

I believe it is immensely helpful for people, especially children, to have a wise mentor and positive role model. We are all conditioned to some extent by the people and the environment we grow up with. This book offers some very practical ideas on how to raise children to live more positive, healthy and productive lives.
– **John Murphy, Best-selling author and transformational leader**

PROMOTING STUDENT SUCCESS

WHAT ARE MY ROLES AS A PARENT

———————

Kelly I. Benedict

Dedication

To my parents Mr and Mrs Benedict, I am grateful for your love, persistence, care and the relevant values you taught me about life.

To all parents, guardians, and teachers I applaud you for your continued efforts towards enhancing the well-being and future of children, who, as global citizens, are the leaders of our tomorrow.

Contents

Acknowledgements

In writing this book, I have beckoned on the skills of many professionals and friends. I would particularly thank:

Virginia who proofread and edited the manuscript, Annie Mebaley, Rena Zeine, Dion C. Jordan, Okeomah, Innocent, Emeka, Allen Annett, Daniel Oluwaseun, Nick Anderson, Amara, Kingsley, Onyekachi, Venicia, Nisomi for your encouragements, all the parents who shared their experience and many others for your support and contributions. Most importantly, I am grateful to God for his grace and wisdom to finish this book.

Introduction

Families are the unit of the society; great families result in great societies. Change begins right at home. If we intend to contribute to the development of our nation, then we should start from the people within our direct control—our family.

The struggle to groom responsible, brilliant and respectful children is real. It's never an easy journey. How will parents do and be their best? What does a successful parent do differently? And how can we get it right as parents? Every parent desires to live a balanced life; to excel at work, be the best spouse and be 100% available for their kids. Is this desire attainable?

YES IT IS.

With you in mind, I have intelligently written ***Promoting Student Success.***

I was a victim of constant academic failure in my teen years. In a class of fifty students, my end of the term academic position would be forty-nine out of fifty. Each time I watch other students celebrate their good grades, I fall into utter despair. I wonder if we descend from the same universe. I regularly asked myself "would I ever excel like other students?"

Perhaps, you are asking the same question concerning your child.

At some point, I had to quit school because I lost interest. But thanks to my parents who encouraged me not to give up.

They said, "You will never become a failure in life until you stop trying."

Hearing this inspiring word, I was determined to excel in all aspects of life. Parents, I clearly understand the frustration of being bottom of the class. However, I pulled through mainly because of my supportive parents. Today, I am an author, advisory to business leaders, parents coach and founder of child initiatives. That is why I offer you practical insights and real life instances of how to be the best parent to your child.

Your child is priceless, and deserves to get the best from you. How would you feel in the next 30 years, if your child becomes the reputable man or woman you wished for? How would you feel to watch your child accomplish their dreams? You will definitely feel fulfilled.

Therefore, never give up on your child. Although your child may start small doesn't mean he or she is an average student. We cannot use their current academic performance to judge their future. Inside your child lies hidden potentials and greatness. Don't focus on their weaknesses rather their unique strengths. I have this confident that, if I can succeed despite my initial limitations your child has a bright future.

In only Five chapters, this timely book reveals power keys to help you bring out the best in your child. I have also added real life instances from parents I interviewed from different parts of the world.

More so, at the end of each chapter are ***action points*** that will prompt you to take a step towards bettering your child's life.

- Chapter 1 concentrates on the ***family***. It describes how the family plays a significant role in your child's life.

- Chapter 2 dwells on ***education.*** It helps you understand the challenges your child face in their academics and how to help your child tackle the challenge and attain maximum success.

- Chapter 3 focuses on ***career.*** Learn how to avoid forcing your dreams on your child and how to help your child pursue their passions professionally.

- Chapter 4 centers on your child's ***future.*** It teaches you how to prepare your child for the future. It also includes the teacher's role in your child's future.

- Chapter 5 teaches about ***values.*** Your child emulates your character. They watch and learn from you. What value would you rather teach them? This chapter carefully explains the importance of training your child in the right value system.

This book is essential for parents, teachers, mentors, coaches, and every individual who seeks to better a child's life.

CHAPTER 1

Family

Laying the Foundation for a Positive Impact

Raising excellent children is a universal desire of all parents. Our goal as parents is to see our children excel beyond our personal achievements and success. These includes, but not limited to building a good family, giving them the best education we can afford, and guiding them through their career path, for the purpose of establishing a great future with fulfilling happiness. Unfortunately, most parents struggle to realize their expectations and desires. The fundamental question remains:

Why do certain children find it difficult to thrive academically and in life general? Why do other children succeed stressfully? And why should we consider laying a good foundation for our children?

Foundation is the groundwork for everything in life. It is the base on which something stands. How you lay the foundation, affects your child hugely.

Architect, engineers and builders understand this when designing a house and laying the foundation for a structure. They know that the shape, design, height and longevity of any building are dependent upon its foundation. In effect, they do their best to ensure the foundation is in perfect condition to carry the entire load of that structure.

- Parents, if an engineer can devote hundred percent attention to buildings, how much more that of your children?

- Have you laid a solid foundation that guarantees success for your children?

- What hinders you from being best parents?

- What should you start doing to build a wonderful family for your children?

As foundations are essential to buildings, so it is in families. Family have been considered, since the beginning of civilisation, to be the strongest pillar of society, just like religion, school, organizations, and associations.

Family is the framework within which socialization, training, and education are made available for children. This makes you parents, the first teachers of your child, a role model and as such you have much influence in affecting your child's long range aspirations, personal development, and expectations in life.

Few years ago, I was invited to represent my school and country in an international conference themed "Innovative Solutions to Global Challenges," which was organised by Higher College of Technology, Dubai. Some of the keynote speakers were Rt. Hon. Tony Blair, former Prime Minister of United Kingdom, Nahayn Mabarak AI Nahyan, Minister of Higher Education UAE and H.H. Sheikh Mohammed bin Rashid AI Maktoum, Vice President and Prime Minister of the UAE and Ruler of Dubai etc.

In one of the forums, there was a young girl; Adora Svitak, who had written a book at the age of four. According to her website, she delivered the speech "What Adults Can Learn from Kids" at TED. The speech received over 3.3 million views on TED.com alone, and has been translated into over forty different languages.

After the conference and during my flight home, I spent hours thinking of Adora's commitment to add value to humanity. How was she able to accomplish such a great impact despite her age and lack of experience? Although she might have been passionate and driven to make a difference, none of this would have been possible, if it were not for her parent's influence, which enabled her reach her goals and make a positive impact globally.

Parents, the fundamental basis for influencing your children begin with your relationship with them, regardless of their age.

- How is the relationship between you and your children?

- Does this relationship add value to their lives in a positive way?

- What effort can you make to be a great parent and role model to your children?

- Your child can be their best if you are willing to give them your best.

The experience I had with Adora made me realize that we cannot successfully discuss "Promoting Student Success" without understanding the foundations necessary for a student to succeed both personally and academically. The kind of foundation we lay as parents in bringing up our children will determine their success in life.

Building a concrete foundation for your child

Growing up as a teenager was difficult, because I faced many challenges; balancing peer pressures, academic performance and my inability to discover my purpose early in life. Based on my experience, I will be sharing certain nuggets of wisdom you can use for your children. The following are some of the tips necessary in building an effective foundation for your children.

Family Security: Never Leave Them Alone

Far more important than financial necessities, children need, the attention, affection, consideration; appreciation, values, and love that help them define their sense of identity. The frequent failures witnessed in high schools can often be explained by the absence or the breach of the emotional balance required for healthy development of students into maturity.

Focusing on the issues at hand and the challenges:

- Frequent quarrels between parents, physical abuse, alcohol addiction, divorce, and radical change of lifestyle, are few examples of factors that could easily threaten the equilibrium a child needs for learning and effective studying.

- Many teenagers who are victims of lack of attention or proper guidance focus their energy on everything that is not related to school. Such as; sex, alcohol, drugs. Simply to seek attention.

- Their failures unconsciously become a cry for help, a means to trigger interest, and a way to indicate that they still matter.

How do you manage these challenges?

- Your child wants to know what is going on. They want to know the status of their relationships, and the changes that will impact their social life at school and at home. And how they are expected to cope with the stress in the environments they live in, and how to avoid derailing from their desired path.

- They want to know how to fit in. They want to know how to cope successfully with peer pressures.

- They don't want to miss out. Teenage years are a very challenging and trying period. Too many things are vying for their attention and they don't want to miss out. How can we parents come to their aid?

- As parents, never leave them alone. They need your attention. Get inside their environment to guide, correct, listen, and instruct them in the best way to live.

A Parent, a Guide, and a Friend

If you are interested in your child's schooling, you should also be actively involved in their academic performance, challenges, extracurricular activities, social life, peer pressures and other personal issues.

Talk with your child about school, discuss with them about their friends, find out the activities they are involved in. This will breed an atmosphere for bonding. More so, your child will trust you enough to share their aspirations, difficulties, and fears.

What should parents do?

The following are a few suggestions from other parents:

- You should certainly be friendly with your child. Your role as parents requires much more than friendship. Friends can offer advice, then back away to allow their friend do what they want. With children, it's different. You need to help them learn how to be disciplined and responsible.

- Your role as parents also includes; mentoring, guiding and listening to your child. You cannot always be a pal, but they should know that you will always be there to support, protect, and defend them and that your love for them is unconditional.

- You should be involved in every aspect of their life. Know who their friends are; protect them from bad influence.

- The truth is; your child will make mistakes. Try not to be judgemental. Coach them instead with unconditional love. That way, they can reach out to you for help.

Your ability to play a role as a parent, friend, and guide to your child makes you an exceptional parent. These three elements allow you build a solid relationship with your child, understanding their needs and finding ways to meet them effectively.

Playing the Role of Mentor

According to *Merriam Webster* dictionary, mentor means "Someone who teaches or gives help and advice to less experienced and often younger person." In this context, it is referring to parents mentoring their children.

As a mentor:

- You should provide information regarding various aspects of life, teach your child about life and facts that may be important to them in the society and the world at large.

- You should seek to share with them; essential wisdom that will guide them in making appropriate choices in life.

Why does your child need a mentor?

Teenage years can be very challenging because of peer pressures and other issues. Every passing second, your child is introduced to new things; through television, magazines, friends and social media.

Each of these elements could influence their lives either positively or negatively. Your role is to clarify their thoughts, listen to their struggles and provide answers to their problems.

Aside being a mentor to your child, there are other exemplary personalities who can mentor your child from afar; through books. I was influenced through the books of these mentors. They include: Dr. David Oyedepo, Zig Ziglar, T. D. Jakes, and David Abioye etc. They are indeed great mentors and leaders. Their books taught me essential life lessons. Such as; the need to accept responsibility, be relevant in the society, maximize my youthful age, and how our choices today determine our future success.

As parents, how well do you know your child's issues, fears and challenges? What step would you take to ensure your child's needs are met?

Lead by Example: Walk the Talk

It's important to note that children always emulate those watching over them. Their behaviour is not random; it is carefully copied. Parents are usually the first individuals they imitate. It explains why the intellectual similarities between parents and their children are just as common as the physical ones.

It is fruitless for parents to expect their child to magically become voracious readers, if they themselves, prioritise watching TV for uninterrupted hours over purchasing books.

- The presence of books and children's familiarity with them will initially spark the curious desire to browse, but then, it will gradually instil a habit of reading.

- Walking the talk was one of the key traits I learned from my father, Mr. Benedict. He's a man of integrity, a man of his word; circumstances don't alter his stand or who he is. When I was a teenager, his lifestyle positively affected my life. I grew up wanting to be like him.

- As a parent, let's examine ourselves; is our lifestyle today worth emulating by our children? If not, what can we do to improve for the benefit of our children's future?

Balancing Work and Family

In the movie *Courageous*, four men had a calling to serve and protect the street as law enforcement officers. These men were committed, confident, and focused on their job. Until one day, when they faced a tough challenge none of them was ready for- fatherhood. When tragedy hits home, Adam Mitchell loses his daughter. Adam and his colleagues are left wrestling with their fears, hopes, faith, and fathering. Six weeks after the incident, Adam prepares a new resolution of what it meant to be a better father; taking full responsibility for his wife and his son, to provide and protect them.

This incident further made Adam realise he wasn't spending enough time with his children, and that to become an effective parent, there was a need to balance work and family responsibilities. If our commitment and dedication for one is higher, it will definitely affect the success of the other.

Despite Adam's tight schedule at work, he made a decision to create time and go for morning runs with his son, as a way to be part of his son's life. As a result, this little act brought a major transformation to Adam's family. It enabled him achieve his resolution to become a better father.

As parents, we don't have to wait for a tragedy to strike before we fulfil our parenting roles. Our children are our greatest treasure. It's our level of responsibility including our time, resources and mentorship that determines their success in life.

I once interviewed a businesswoman, and asked what her ultimate goal in life was. She said "My greatest desire is not only being successful in my career, but to be a successful mother to my kids and a good wife to my husband."

In my view, that's a true success, winning in your career as well as with your family.

Real Life Examples to Emulate

In the course of writing this book, I was privileged to interview other parents, who shared their perspective about balancing work and family life. The analysis of their feedback shows that today, our lives, and the lives of our children, are structured in such a way that there is little or no time to just relax and be without thinking of what comes next on our life's agenda.

How did other parents balance their work and family successfully? Let's see what these parents have to say:

- I was in a high-pressure job as a senior manager, working long hours. For years, any spare time I had, I spent with my children, at the expense of having time for myself or my friends. Kids have to be prioritised, and for that we need to make time for them.

- It is essential to create and maintain the opportunity and prioritisation for time that is focused on the family, including your husband or wife, as well as the children. Maintaining a strong and positive relationship with your husband or wife is one of the best things you can do for the self-esteem and the success of your children.

- If both parents work, see to it that mum and dad both take time off to be there for the kids. Try to adjust your working hours when possible. Realise that actively spending time with your kids is better for their future and yours as a parent than only working. Value yourself as an adult and parent in such a way that you would rather invest time in your kids than only in your work.

- Put the child's interests ahead of your own. It is only for a few years and a chance you will never have again. As a parent, it is something you can do.

- Each person's situation is different, but what is critical is that the time we do spend with our children should be quality time. Be present and not on your phone or e-mail. Even if we have extremely limited time, the conversations we have with our children need to clearly identify our love and support for them.

Family ~ Action Points

- What is your child's current lifestyle?
- What major steps can you take today to bring out the best in their life?
- What would you stop doing and what can you start doing? In order to be great parents to them?

CHAPTER 2

Education

Stability of the Future and your Commitment as Parents

Education is the bedrock for a stable future and prosperity. Before I travelled to the city to attend high school and pursue a degree abroad, I represented my school and country at a conference in Dubai and the United States of America. I learned that in every corner of the world, families are undoubtedly different; they do not have access to the same privileges and opportunities. They do not experience the same difficulties and do not necessarily hold the same values and beliefs.

However, I have found an indisputable common ground; it is the pursuit of academic and professional success for their children.

Even in remote areas, where decent financial means are not always available in most families, parents never cease to work hard to support their children through school. Not only because education is unequivocally essential, but because children ultimately become their parents' glory.

To illustrate this, think of African societies in which the following scenario is rather frequent:

When a child is recognized as intelligent and well mannered, people always ask after their parents. "Who are his parents?" they inquire. People honour the parents rather than just the child alone.

Education and Children's Challenges

In today's world, despite our parental commitments, responsibilities, and other personal efforts to ensure our children go to school, there are still some fundamental challenges most children face.

The truth about your child's education

Unfortunately, many parents tend to abandon their children's academic progress as soon as they have completed their school registration, when instead, we should continue to help them find their deepest motivations till they attain a physical, mental, intellectual and spiritual sovereignty.

This is what, in my opinion, partially explains the loss of motivation in most high school students and this continues to rise in alarming rates. More and more students are losing interest in learning and succeeding in school, and we parents often do not realise the need for our intervention.

Understandably, many of us find it difficult to get involved in our children's academics because of the complexity of our own adult lives. We lack the time to assume all of our obligations because we are too busy making money for their education.

But despite this reality, we must take charge of some basic tasks in order to promote their education. Such responsibility is too heavy and can't just be dumped on the teachers' shoulders alone.

What is the way forward?

In his speech "Future Education: High School and College Educational Trends—Preparing Students for Life," Dr. Patrick Dixon made a profound statement, "We either take hold of our future or the future takes hold of us." What does this mean? You are the first educator and history maker of your children, while teachers are the history creator for them.

Teachers are building a future in the lives of students they teach. I agree with Dr. Patrick, if we are going to educate and impact the lives of our children, we need to start thinking about some fundamental questions:

- What are we actually preparing our children for?

- In what ways can we make education more fun and interesting for them?

- How do we create an inspiring learning environment?

- How can we get involved to support and encourage our children to succeed and reach their ultimate goals in life?

This fundamental role begins when parents and teachers play important and complementary roles in their education. The influence of both parties is significant to fully ensure a child's development in all stages of their life.

I believe every child would be better off, if we parent attempt to follow these few suggestions.

Give Meaning to Your Child's Education

For ever-growing empowerment, whenever a student is at crossroads; where he seeks to decide the right path to choose to reach his personal goals, and how to do well in school for himself, not just for his parents. The key is to help him create a powerful bond between the student he is now and the adult he aspires to be. This will teach him to envision himself opening golden doors of triumph someday.

To give meaning to your child's education, you should consider these examples:

- If a student wants to become an automotive engineer, parents ought to find a way to make it fun and encourage them at an early stage.

  In sharing an interesting story about his son, one parent said, "Children are sentient beings. They should not be condescended or underestimated. I remember when my oldest son was three years old and was very curious about the automobile. I took him through the entire system, from the fuel tank to the exhaust. He had no difficulty comprehending."

- What if the student is a lover of words and imagines himself as a writer?

  Based on experience, the best thing to do is help him discover his areas of interest, and then purchase materials related to those topics. Encourage him to read, improve his vocabulary, and hone his writing skills. Teach him basic writing skills, such as structuring his ideas, grammar and knowing his target audience.

  More so, it's not necessarily about locking him into an intangible project, but helping him maximize his efforts towards academic excellence.

Getting Involved in Your Child's Education

Oftentimes, we yell at our children as a way to punish them for their poor academic performance. Instead of that, empower them to focus on learning and improving. The practice of teaching by humiliating your child degrades and disables them.

While acknowledging that your child needs help with certain learning objectives, it is also very important to build their self-esteem by recognising their strengths. Are they passionate about Literature, arts, geography, music and sports? Contrary to popular belief, these subjects that are thought as common are actually very valuable.

No field of study should be denigrated, no matter what value society places on that field. A student might be talented in such an area, that he effortlessly succeeds and attain deep fulfilment. All we need do is to give them the necessary support required to reach their desired goals.

How Can Parents Get Involved?

You can take the following steps to address the problems of your child's poor academic performance in certain subjects.

Kelly Benedict Child Support Initiative – GUIDE Model	
Parent-Child Performances Tool	
Step 1: Guide Your Child	**Step 2: Understand Your Child**
■ Assess your child's overall performance, including present and the past results. Excellent Good Average Poor 90% 60% 50% 40% ■ Why is your child struggling academically? ■ What is the reason behind their poor academic performance? ■ Ponder on those questions	■ Create time to discuss with your child; talk about their academic strengths and weaknesses. ■ Identify those issues your child faces academically. ■ Proceed to step three to know where they need help.
Step 3: Invest in Your Child	**Step 4: Teach Diligence to Your Child**
■ Would your child need additional learning materials based on their academic issues? ■ Does this require you enrolling your child in summer classes or extra classes? ■ Would your child need your personal assistance or teacher's support? ■ Ensure that you provide all the necessary support.	■ Teach your child the importance of hard-work and its reward. ■ Inform them why personal responsibility is the key to success in all aspects of life. ■ Let them know that diligence means reading their books, doing their assignment on time, preparing for their exams and assessment tests in advance.

Kelly Benedict Child Support Initiative – GUIDE Model Parent-Child Performances Tool	
Step 5: Encourage Your Child	**Key Thought**
<ul><li>Let your child know that you believe in them despite their academic performance.</li><li>Let them know that it doesn't matter how they started, rather they should stay focused and work hard.</li><li>Encourage your child with words such as; we believe in you. Don't give up hope. Keep trying. Your best is ahead. You are destined to succeed.</li></ul>	<ul><li>Parents if you would apply these steps correctly and consistently, your child would not only improve academically but they can also become an excellent and award winning student.</li></ul>

Monitoring and Celebrating Their Academic Success

To create sustainable success, ensure you monitor and celebrate your child's academic progress. How can you accomplish this? Let's consider the following tips:

Monitoring their progress

- You should endeavour to see your child's performance. This begins by playing the role of coach, by gently but persistently nudging them in the direction of their targets and by encouraging them daily.

- Always check their books after school to ensure they are on the right track.

- Get involved in their subjects to understand areas where they need help and how they can receive this help.

- Teach them how to manage their time by striking a balance between their academics and other activities.

- Help them choose the right associates; by always providing guidance.

Celebrating their performance

- Uplift and encourage them by celebrating every bit of progress they make.

- Avoid criticism, especially to a low-performing student, because when you criticise, you degrade their morale.

- Don't judge them with their current results. Rather, tell them who they can become.

- Reward them with gifts as a way to motivate and sustain their success.

Real Life Examples to Emulate

If you ever think of giving up on your child because of their poor educational performance, read my personal story. I became a successful student despite initial limitations. So what were my experiences, struggles, and challenges?

My experience:

All through primary school, I didn't have any interest in school. My greatest desires then were to drop out of school and begin a career in farming. I was interested in cracking palm kernel. At a point, I quit school and spent almost a year at home doing nothing. But my parents kept up with their encouragement despite my limitations. As parents, your child's poor academic performance doesn't matter; keep encouraging them not to give up until they reach their academic success.

My struggles:

After primary school, I managed to attend secondary school. But the struggle continued; I had difficulties in my studies due to poor academic performance. I was always bottom of the class. I was discouraged and thought that I wasn't destined to be the best at school. However, in my final senior secondary English examination, I got a pass grade and things took a different turn.

My breakthrough:

My breakthrough came after my parents encouraged me to attend a youth program organised by Winners Chapel, "Canaan land" Lagos. The things I heard impacted me and changed my view of the world. I started seeing myself as an excellent student, no longer as an average student. Remember this; what we say to our children can affect their lives positively or negatively. I experienced change because I heard the right things at the right time and it impacted my life. What do you often say to your child? Are they encouraging words?

What if you start saying, "My child, you are destined to win, I know you can do it. I believe in you, and I will be there for you?"

My responsibility:

After the event, I made a decision to work hard and be one of the top students. Remember that achieving academic excellence is not determined by our family background. Rather, excellence is a product of hard work. The true definition of hard work is accepting responsibility. Responsibility is the cost paid to achieve greatness. So teach your child how to accept responsibility, both academically and in life generally. At the end of my degree program, I was among the top students, represented my school internationally, and today, an author of books. It became possible because I accepted responsibility. If I could become an author, your child can accomplish their dreams.

My success:

I am grateful to God, because none of this would be possible if it wasn't for His grace. When I look at where I used to be, where I am today, and where I am going, I can boldly say "there is no dull child." Every child is destined to succeed. This is why I would advise; don't judge your child based on their current performance at school, rather remind them who they can become. Your role as parents is to encourage, support, and be there for your child, especially in times when they need you the most.

Education ~ Action Points

- Parents, how is your child's current academic performance?

- What can you do to strike a balance between your work and family so you can study with your child, encourage and support them?

- When your child improves their academic performance, what kind of gift or encouragement can you give them as a way to boost their momentum?

CHAPTER 3

Career

Encourage Them to Pursue Their Dreams: Cultivate Options

Cultivating options and encouraging your children's dreams describes the story of Richard Williams, father of world-class tennis players Serena and Venus Williams. The story is told that Richard loved tennis and dreamed someday that he would watch his children play professionally. Although Richard had little success working with Serena and Venus's three older sisters, Serena and Venus took to the game immediately.

According to Sports JRank, in 1991, Richard sent Serena and Venus off to Florida to train at the tennis academy of Ric Macci in Delray Beach. Both girls turned professional by the age of fourteen and have been guided by their father through every step of their careers.

Why did Richard make such commitment?

Richard William shows us that the ultimate goal of every parent is to see their children happy, doing what they love, and being successful. Because of his commitment, encouragement, and coaching of his two daughters, today they are happily pursuing their passion and making an impact around the world as tennis legends.

Your child does not have to be like Serena and Venus, but all children have hidden talents and passions. All you need is to give them the necessary support to actualize their dream, like Richard did for his daughters.

The challenges of dreaming for your child

What happens if you fail to encourage your child to pursue his dreams but instead impose your personal desires on them?

- Your child will lose interest studying the course in the school.

- He will lack the zeal and commitment to stay focused.

- When he faces challenges, there's a tendency to give up.

- The only reason he's doing this activity is to please you, but it is not his aspiration and dream.

- He will struggle to succeed because he lacks the strength and passion needed to achieve excellence.

In 2008, I had a similar experience when I got admission to an educational institution abroad to further my degree program. I was advised to study Software Engineering or other Information Technology (IT) related courses, since IT was in high demand in the job market. Although I did well academically, I didn't have any sense of fulfilment.

After completing the program, I realised I did not have much interest in IT, so I decided to pursue my passion. Imagine the time spent, the resources, and what could have happened if my degree course had been connected to my passion? I would have achieved greater success and fulfilment.

I heard a story of a man and his wife, who asked their son to become a medical doctor. He consented; because he wanted to please his parents. However, after he graduated from medical school, he gave his certificate to them and said "I have fulfilled your dreams. I'll go ahead and pursue mine."

Life is too short to waste our resources and time trying to impose our dreams on our children, especially if they do not have interest in the same area. To avoid such mistakes, consider the following suggestions:

Don't Force Your Dreams on Your Child

From strengths to weaknesses, every human is singularly different. Expecting an adolescent with personal issues arising constantly to excel in everything will lead to eventual disappointment for the parents. But most importantly, it will lead to an avoidable loss of self-confidence in your children.

What role should parent play?

- You must acknowledge your child as they are, and accept what your child strives to be in life.

- This helps to avoid forcing your personal desires on them and confusing your own educational desires with your child's educational path.

- Parents should at all times, encourage their children to dream for themselves. This leads a child to seek not just a good career, but one that is fulfilling, which in turn, allows them to achieve greater success and have a joyful life.

Discovering Your Child's Dream Early

The best gift you can give to your children is to guide and help them discover their passion and dream early in life. This enables them to avoid future mistakes.

How Do You Guide Your Child?

You should consider the following tips

1.	**Pay Attention To Your Child**	■ As your child grows from childhood to adolescence, you should pay adequate and close attention to him/her.
2.	**Watch Your Child**	■ Don't force your dream on your child but through your observation, find out: ■ What career endeavour excites your child the most? ■ What can your child do very well without formal training? ■ What would your child love to do even if there were no financial rewards? ■ This could be a clue to discovering your child's passion.
3.	**Interact With Your Child**	■ Observation isn't enough; you should create time to discuss with your child about their future aspirations.
4.	**Understand Your Child**	■ Your child is unique and cannot be everything. Focus on his academic strengths rather than his weaknesses.
5.	**Believe In Your Child**	■ Let your child be aware that Dad and Mum believe in him.
6.	**Support Your Child**	■ Provide all the necessary support your child may need to succeed both personally and academically.

7.	**Mentor Your Child**	■ Share experiences and examples of how others succeed with your child.
8.	**Connect Your Child To Professionals**	■ Look out for professionals who have undertaken similar career paths and introduce them to your child.
9.	**Motivate Your Child**	■ Speak encouraging and inspiring words to your child because encouragement is fundamental for success.
10.	**Be Patient With Your Child**	■ Success takes time. You need to be patient with your child for them to reach their desired goals.
11.	**Guide Your Child**	■ Guide your child especially in the area of his character, associations, and their lifestyle to ensure he lives an excellent life.
12.	**Celebrate Your Child**	■ Celebrate every progress your child makes whether personally or academically.

Inspire Them to Pursue Their Passions in Developing Their Profession

In this twenty-first century, nobody cares much about whether you are educated or not. This doesn't mean that education is not relevant. Of course it is, but things are changing. For instance, where someone studied doesn't count as much as:

- What he can do as a person

- The problem he can solve

- The ideas he can generate

- The change he can bring

- The value he can add to humanity

Just because a child may not be a high performer academically doesn't mean they are inadequate. There are other areas with their passions and talents, where they can perform better.

This passion or talent could be the major catalyst toward reaching their destiny in life. I'm a perfect example of this. As I shared earlier, when I discovered my passion for writing, I decided to pursue it with all diligence. And today, I'm the author of several books that is impacting lives globally.

What is passion?

Passion is something we love doing even if there's no financial attachment. It can be our hobbies or something that interests us and brings excitement whenever we do it. This passion differs from one person to another. For some, their passion could be football, for others, its music, fashion, or any other area.

What can you do to help kindle your child's passion?

- Help them turn their passion into a profession.

- Help them run the race of pursuing their passion.

- Encourage and support them whenever they need help.

- Connect them with people who make a living in those passions.

- Believe in them and let them know they can do it, regardless of the challenges they face.

Real Life Examples to Emulate

To help your child discover their passions and dreams, consider the following examples from other parents:

- Keep trying different activities with your kids as they grow up. For instance, try a mix of sports, music, dance, debate, and others. This allows you see where their talents and interests are. Once you are able to discover this with your child, encourage them in that direction. Work with them to learn the requirements needed to accomplish their dreams. Your complete support will help your child succeed.

- Recognise that each child will have his or her own passion and that they are not here to live out our own unfulfilled dreams. Although we might want our children to do what we would have liked to do or to follow our footsteps, we need to understand that children need to explore their own desires and needs to figure out what they are interested in.

- We should manage our expectations and not make our children feel we are disappointed especially when they decide to follow their dreams. Be excited, encouraging, and supportive in any field they choose to pursue.

- Our children are independent individuals and should be respected and seen as such. As much as you would like your child to make some of the choices you made, do your best to encourage them in their path. Our children's life choices need to be made by them, not by us. The only time you should intervene is when their choice could be harmful to them and to others.

- Let them explore their ideas and visions and be creative. It will teach them that one can succeed and sometimes fail, but the idea to explore is important. Never tell them what to be; instead, allow them choose from the options available in the world. Teach them to work hard at it to succeed.

Career ~ Action Points

Do you know your child's passions, interests, and talents (PIT)?
Consider these questions:

- **Passion** – what captures your child's attention and he/she will be happy to do it if they have the resources?
- **Interest** – what type of career endeavor excites your child most?
- **Talent** – what can your child do very well and effortlessly, without formal training?

When you discover their PIT, what ways can you support and inspire them to accomplish their set goals?

CHAPTER 4

Future

Today Child, Tomorrow Adult: From Eaglet to Eagle

The eagle is one of the largest and most powerful predatory birds and it's known for its glory and strength. The eagle is a symbol of courage and power because of its large size and the inaccessibility of its nest. The eagle does not struggle to flap its wings; it takes advantage of the direction of the wind to make flight effortless. Eagles take forty days every year to renew their feathers in order to maintain better flight. But what happens when an eaglet loses its identity?

The Rediscovery of the Eaglet's Identity

In the article *The Eagle,* Nancy Missler shares a story about a lost eaglet. This story offers interesting lessons and also models strategies for success we can teach our children as they prepare to attain future stability as adults.

Let's examine this story

Once upon a time, walking through the forest, a farmer found an eaglet lying on the ground. It was wounded and dying. Out of pity, he picked it up and took it home. He kept it in the chicken coop in his barn, with his chickens. Soon, the eaglet learned to eat chicken food and behave like a chicken.

Many days later, a bird naturalist happened to visit the farmer's chicken coop. When he saw the eaglet eating worms and grain and living on the farm, he was surprised and asked the farmer, "Why is there an eaglet living with your chickens? The eagle is the king of birds. Eagles are meant to fly, not to live on farms and eat chicken food!"

The farmer replied, "What else could I do? I found it in the forest when it was very small, and I felt bad for it. I picked it up and kept it in my barn. It grew up here, and it looks quite happy being one of the chicks."

The naturalist retorted, "My dear friend, you are mistaken; an eagle is an eagle. We have to teach this eaglet how to fly. It has to realise its potential and qualities. Only by using them to the fullest will it find true happiness and fulfilment."

Immediately, the naturalist picked the eaglet up in his hands and tried to teach him to fly. But it was in vain! The eaglet would not even open its wings. It was afraid of flying and did not even know it could fly!

Again, the naturalist lifted the eaglet from the ground. This time, he kept the eaglet high above his head. Patiently, he kept saying, "You belong to the sky. Look at the heavens; look up there. Open your wings and begin to fly."

The eaglet was confused and scared. When the eaglet saw the chickens eating their food on the ground, he dropped heavily to the ground and joined them. The naturalist did not give up. He knew that in spite of the evidence, inside that bird was an eagle's heart throbbing for greatness and longing for excellence.

The next day at sunrise, the naturalist took the eaglet and went to the top of a small mountain nearby and patiently began encouraging the frightened bird to fly. He kept telling the bird, "Fly, fly, dear eaglet. Open your wings. Climb the heights, forget the chicken barn below. Fly! Fly!" And without much ado, he flung the bird up toward the sky. The eaglet, unaware of his unknown self and afraid of the height, shivered with fear and allowed himself to drop down. He was now on the side of a cliff on the mountain, gazing at the farmhouse down below in the valley!

Then the naturalist made the eaglet face the rays of the rising sun. Lovingly, he kept telling the eaglet, "Realise your greatness. You are not a chick; you are an eagle!

You can fly. The sky is your fatherland. The heights are calling you. You are not meant for the earth. Open, open your wings. Dare to fly!"

Finally, the eaglet stared at the brightness of the rising sun. Its warmth caressed its wings. Its piercing brightness stabbed its heart. Something awoke in its soul. All of a sudden, the eaglet trembled, shook all over, and slowly, his wings expanded. Then they fluttered. At last, with its eyes glued to the radiant sun, the eaglet majestically rose from the ground and flew. It hastened his speed, soaring higher and higher till it reached the inaccessible heights of the heavens!

Relating the Story to Your Child's Life

What does this story mean to you as parents? How does this story relate to your child's life?

In this story, there are three main characters, the eaglet (your child), the farmer (their teacher), and the naturalist (you as a parent). Each one's roles and responsibilities differ. For instance, it doesn't matter how expensive and reputable your child's school may be, their teachers will always perform their duty at some point. Yet, just as the farmer couldn't help the eaglet much, teachers cannot teach everything to your child. There are still fundamental roles you ought to play to help your child attain their dreams in life.

What are these fundamental truths?

- **Help them see.** The best gift you can give to your child is to help them see, to discover who they are, what they can do and what they are destined to be. Remember the first thing the naturalist did was ask, "Why is there an eaglet living with your chickens?" He was able to see what the eaglet was meant to be—the king of birds, not a chicken. Your child needs to be aware that he is not an average student or failure, rather an excellent student.

- **Speak into their life.** You have to be like the naturalist who constantly told the eaglet, "Realise your greatness. You are not a chick; you are an eagle! You can fly." Parents, it is high time you speak to your child about their destiny, education, and success. Your role is to help your child realise the greatness within them. This can only be done when you speak successful messages, such as, "You belong at the top, don't give up hope. You can do it; we believe you can, and you have what it takes to succeed in life."

- **Be an encourager.** Every child desires greatness and longs for excellence. But if your child is not performing well at school, or not meeting targets as you expect, always remember that success does not happen overnight and it does not come by accident. Success takes time. Therefore, encourage them by reminding them that their best is ahead. Focus more on their progress rather than their weaknesses.

- **Be patient.** You need to be patient, like the naturalist, in order to accomplish this greatness in your child's life. Patience is not how long it takes for training or guiding your child to succeed, but rather your willingness to endure until he or she reaches their dreams.

- **Be a guide.** The naturalist asked the farmer why an eagle resided with chickens. Many parents are surprised at the kind of habits their children display or the company they keep. For instance, the reason why the eaglet found itself in the midst of chickens was because it lacked the guidance of its eagle parents. This implies that when your child is not properly guided, they can easily be influenced by the wrong company.

- **Be present.** It is important to provide your child's basic needs, but your presence in their lives makes an enormous difference. Teachers often ask what they can do, but the truth is no one other than you can teach your child how to fly. Apart from bringing food home for the eaglet, the mother or father eagle also creates time to teach their young eaglet how to fly. This goes on for a period of time until the eaglet starts flapping its wings. In as much as we provide material things for our children, how well do you know your child's needs? Maybe they need clarity about certain things or someone to talk to. What effort can you make to ensure that these needs are met?

How About Today's Child, Tomorrow's Adult?

Parents should appreciate this truth; life is about stages and processes. We all undergo these processes. It is essential to establish a very strong foundation for your children to effectively transit from childhood to adolescence and then to adulthood. Let's consider some of these life stages.

- **Childhood.** The childhood stage is largely about nurturing and protecting the child from themselves and others. Childhood is also a learning period for your children. Pay close attention to their desires and aspirations by playing with them, sitting with them, hearing them out, taking interest in their daily life, as well as explaining things to them when asked. As scripture says" Train up a child in the way he should go and when he is old, he will not depart from it."

- **Adolescence.** A parent's role change as the child grows, developing their own identity, capacity, advancing physically, mentally, and emotionally.

At this stage, they want to explore their dreams, abilities, and potentials. We should advise, inform, and support them in making right decisions. Our role as parents is not only to give our children the tools to be grounded and become responsible adolescents, but also to model the behaviours and values we are trying to teach them.

- **Adulthood.** Adulthood is a very complex time for your child. Your role is to give them life examples, especially your own personal experience.

  - What steps did you take to be where you are today?

  - What challenges did you encounter?

  - How were you able to overcome these challenges?

  You might need to create time to share your story with them. Your ability to provide answers to the above questions equips them to avoid similar mistakes. Allowing them fulfil their ultimate dreams in life.

Remember your level of responsibility and commitment in these three stages impacts your children's success.

Preparing Children for the Future: Parents' Role

To prepare your child for their future, consider the following:

- Help them develop a sound mindset; by shaping their moral behaviour, teaching them how to be disciplined, cultured and by teaching them the importance of hard work and its rewards.

- Let there be a constant reminder of who they are, their potentials, talents, and the good qualities they possess.

- Expose them to the right environment, practices and teach them to keep the right company; because it will affect their lives positively.

- Be sensitive enough to observe if they are on the right track or not. This begins with showing concern, drawing them close, and spending quality time with them.

- Expose your child to all aspects of life— academics, sex education, cultures, religions, as well as social and global issues of concern. Share with them both the negative and positive impacts of engaging in any of these areas.

Preparing Children for the Future: Teachers' Roles

While the parent's role is to lay the foundation, teachers build on that foundation for a lasting and sustainable success.

- Schools should restructure or establish a good curriculum that deals specifically with the issues relating to morality, character, emotional well-being, and sense of responsibility, creativity, teamwork, leadership skills, and many other values of good conduct.

- The world is constantly changing, and teachers and schools should move at the same pace to ensure that students are engaged in today's world and can adapt effectively.

- Have a counsellor who handles students' issues and addresses both their personal and educational needs. That way, students won't feel helpless when they need someone to talk to.

Real Life Examples to Emulate

Many parents shared the following views on how to create positive impact for a child's future.

- Critical thinking skills are keys to ensure that children are ready, not only for jobs, but also for changing roles that will come up in the future of our global economy. Most importantly, we need to help our children be adaptable to change.

- Parents have to lead by example and be there when their children fail, as failure needs to be a good lesson. That way, children will be able to make their own decisions in the future.

- We can encourage our children to explore different skills, fields, and occupations. They should not worry about making mistakes; instead they should keep trying out something that is of interests to them.

Future ~ Action Points

- What major roles will you play as your child go through childhood?

- How can you channel their youthful strengths into something meaningful as they enter adolescence?

- How can your life experience be useful to your child, as they learn to trust their decisions and make choices during their adult life?

CHAPTER 5

Values

Essential Values to Teach Your Children: Pillars of Their Destiny

We have learned so much about laying the foundation for our children, giving meaning to their education, encouraging them to follow their dreams, and preparing them for the future. Yet it requires having the right values to establish and sustain any success that is achieved.

Why values are essential

Values are essential in all aspect of life—academically, personally and professionally. I remember vividly that all through my primary and secondary school years, I was not opportune to learn values until I got into the university. On a fateful day, our lecturer, Mrs. Desiree Yap, walked into the classroom and gave us a list of values. She asked us to choose the ones that most mattered to us. Some of these values are integrity, excellence, courage, innovation, character, respect, contentment, patience and diligence etc.

Since then, I see values as the guiding principles and standards in everything I do and how I live. For instance, my highest value academically was excellence, career wise is to be innovative, and personally to be diligent in order to succeed in life and affect others positively. I remain ever grateful to our lecturer for teaching us the importance of values.

Your child might be familiar with those values mentioned, but may not know how to apply them in their own lives. We should ask ourselves:

- What does integrity mean to you as a parent? How can you create time to teach your child the benefits of being a man or woman of integrity?

- What about perseverance? Maybe your child failed many times and wants to quit. Teach them to hold on and try again; doing this will make them understand that "quitters never win, and winners never quit." As quoted Vince Lombardi.

- Every child wants to be a leader. Is leadership about occupying a post? What does it mean to be a leader? What traits must be acquired to be an effective leader and impact lives successfully?

Some of these questions are very important to your children. Parents must be available to answer their children's questions and provide adequate guidance from time to time. It is never too early to teach your child relevant values.

In this chapter, we will examine some of these values. I encourage parents to look for other values that might also be important to you and your child. Let's consider a few.

Learning the Acts of Belonging

In her article, "Create a Sense of Belonging," Karyn Hill defines the sense of belonging as "A human need, just like the need for food and shelter." This is why every human has an inherent desire to belong and be part of something greater than them; someplace they feel loved, cared about, and celebrated. Middle-Earth-Nj observed, "Valuing your teen means giving them a vote in decisions, listening to their input, recognising and using their strengths, and understanding their weaknesses and finding ways to strengthen them."

This not only brings your family together, but also creates a secure relationship and self-assurance for your children. What can you do today to make your home more exciting and loving for your children, wife, or husband?

Cultivating an Attitude of Forgiveness

In as much as we all crave to be part of something, someone might be hurt in the process, either intentionally or unintentionally, through our actions and words. Mayo observed, "Forgiveness doesn't mean that you deny the other person's responsibility for hurting you, and it doesn't minimize or justify the wrong." Rather, forgiveness is our ability to make peace instead of revenge, and having a healthy relationship instead of holding grudges. In effect, teach your children the attitude of forgiveness because being unforgiving has a hold over us.

Embracing the Spirit of Adaptability

Adaptability is another great virtue because it not only prepares your children for excellence, but also teaches them how to adapt to any situation or environment they might find themselves in. Teach them how to stay open to change and not to give up when things are not going as planned, personally and professionally. I'm grateful to my parents for teaching me how to adapt and stay positive in all my endeavours.

The Power of Character: Why it is Essential?

In the course of life, it doesn't matter how skilful or competent someone might be; if they lack character, everything else amounts to nothing. As we often hear, character is everything. The same way salt gives taste to food, character is the true beauty of a man or woman. Teach children the negative and positive consequences of how their lifestyle today could impact their life in the future.

The Benefits of Accepting Responsibility

Responsibility is the price we pay for greatness. Teach your child to be responsible in their families and the society at large. This begins with assigning small tasks like cleaning their rooms, washing dishes and doing other basic household chores. These small responsibilities could be a great foundation in preparing them for success in the future.

The Need to be Organised: Why it is Essential?

One of the greatest challenges some people face today, either at work or in their marriage, is lack of organization, which they didn't cultivate at an early in their lives. Being organised is not limited to composure, timeliness, cleanliness, and accountability, but also the ability to manage our lives efficiently. Teach them the need to be organised as they grow from childhood to adulthood.

Real Life Examples to Emulate

Here are examples of how parents can teach their children the importance of values:

- **The Power of Honesty.** In my home, honesty is at the top of my list. Some refer to it as "being real" or "being genuine." All parents need to show children the importance of being honest. We should not make promises to children that we do not or cannot keep—this teaches them it is ok to not be truthful. When they observe our business or personal dealings with others, they need to be able to discern our honesty within those interactions. Personal and business connections are built on trust, and trust is gained through honesty.

- **The Power of Integrity.** Integrity is about honouring our word. We need to have integrity in our thoughts and actions. Kids are able to pick hypocrisy quickly, when you say one thing and do another. We as parents should be our children's role model. For instance, when taking care of elderly parents, our children learn how to treat the elderly with respect.

- **The Power of Learning.** Be a lifelong learner. Always be willing and eager to learn. Teach your children that learning is valuable and we can always improve if we are humble and curious enough to learn. Openness to learning is an ingredient for your child's success.

- **The Power of Courage.** Teach them how to be courageous in both small and large aspects of life. It is said that courage is the first virtue, without which no other virtues can exist. When things are challenging or when fear arises in our lives, we need to have the courage to move forward, step by step.

- **The Power of Resilience.** Resilience is imperative in today's world. How we pick ourselves up when we've been knocked down. Encourage your child to get back on their feet, when they fail.

- **Be a Role Model.** Kids observe their parents very closely and imitate these qualities, whether good or bad. This implies that, they are influenced by what they watch you do. Set them on a good path, by being a good example.

Values ~ Action Points

What values do you think would suit your child's life? Let's look at the following values and circle all that apply to your child.

Appreciation	Excellent	Learning	Sex
Attitude	Education	Meekness	Self control
Association	Equality	Money	Success
Believe	Focus	Opportunity	Teamwork
Bribe	Faithfulness	Obedience	Timeliness
Commitment	Generosity	Orderliness	Talent
Carelessness	Hope	Persistence	Tolerance
Corruption	Health	Peace	Truth
Contentment	Hospitality	Perception	Unity
Choice	Innovation	Pride	Uniqueness
Diligence	Justice	Punctuality	Vision
Discipline	Kindness	Patience	Violent
Dedication	Knowledge	Quality	Volunteer
Determination	Leadership	Reputation	Wisdom
Empathy	Loyalty	Reliability	Winning

Pick one or two daily and teach your children the importance of adopting the above values in their lives, and how it can positively impact their academic and personal success.

Conclusion

With guidance, coaching and mentoring, all students can attain success and fulfilment in life. As parents, teachers, and members of society, we play a crucial role in nurturing students in discovering their strengths, passion, talents and developing their identities.

Furthermore, we carry the glorious responsibility of helping students succeed academically. The reason is that student motivation and performance can be enhanced by changing the nature of the teacher-student relationships, parent-child connection and designing a more humane organizational culture in schools; specifically, a constructive culture that upholds students' needs and aspirations.

We should constantly envision ourselves and the society in twenty years time, and would see what could be shaped by the collective contributions of today's teenagers. Consequently; today's teenagers are tomorrow's leaders.

Finally, let's remember that there is no average child, regardless of their current academic performance. Every child has the potential to be great, make a difference, realize their dreams and live a happy life, if we can make extra efforts to give them our best support.

Notes

Chapter 1: Family

1. Adora Svitak, accessed 10 May 2015, http://www.adorasvitak.com/about.html

2. *Merriam Webster Online,* mentor, http://www.merriam-webster.com/dictionary/mentor.

3. Alex Kendrick and Stephen Kendrick *Courageous,* directed by Alex Kendrick, (2011, TriStar Pictures, Sherwood Pictures, Provident Films, Affirm Films, and Alabama Production Group).

Chapter 2: Education

1. Dr. Patrick Dixon, "Future Education: High School and College Educational Trend – Preparing Students for Life, accessed 15 July 2015. https://www.youtube.com/watch?v=PU85gPt-4FMY

Chapter 3: Career

1. "Venus and Serena Williams." In *AFRICAN AMERICAN ICONS OF SPORT: Triumph, Courage, and Excellence,* Westport, CT: Greenwood Press, 2008. *The African Ameri-*

canExperience. Greenwood Publishing Group. http://testaae.greenwood.com/doc.aspx?file-ID=GR4028&chapterID=GR4028-1231&path=-books/greenwood. (accessed <11 July 2015>).

2. "Serena Williams – Related Biography: Father/coach Richard Williams," accessed <11 July 2015, http://sports.jrank.org/pages/5326/Williams-Serena-Related-Biography-Father-Coach-Richard-Williams.html.

Chapter 4: Future

1. Nancy Missler, "The Eagle," accessed <7 June 2015>, http://www.ribessj.org/the_eaglet.pdf.

Chapter 5: Values

1. Karyn Hill PhD, "Create A Sense of Belonging," *Pieces of Mind* (blog), *Psychology Today*, March 24, 2014, https://www.psychologytoday.com/blog/pieces-mind/201403/create-sense-belonging.

2. Middle-Earth-Nj, "Providing a Strong Sense of Belonging," *Middle Earth* (blog), April 16, 2012, https://middleearthnj.wordpress.com/2012/04/16/providing-a-strong-sense-of-belonging/.

3. Mayo Clinic, "Forgiveness: Letting go of grudges and bitterness," *Mayo Clinic*, last modified

November 11, 2014, http://www.mayoclinic.org/
healthy-lifestyle/adult-health/in-depth/forgive-
ness/art-20047692.

Conclusion

1. R. Zeine, C.A. Boglarsky, E. Daly, P. Blessinger, M. Kurban, and A. Gilkes. "Considerate Leadership as a Measure of Effectiveness in Medical and Higher Education: Analysis of Supervisory/ Managerial Leadership," *Organizational Cultures: An International Journal*, 15 (1) (2014): 1–13, http://ijmoc.cgpublisher.com/product/ pub.258/prod.55.

2. R. Zeine, F. Palatnick, C.A. Boglarsky, P. Blessinger, B. Herrick, and M.T. Hamlet, "Customer Service Focus and Mission Articulation as measures of Effectiveness in Higher Education Institutions: Driving Student Success." *Management Education: An International Journal*, 14(1) (2014): 1–10, http://ijme.cgpublisher.com/product/pub.252/prod.30.

About the Author

Kelly Benedict is an inspirational author, speaker, advisory to business leaders, parent coach, child advocate and personal development expert—enabling people reach their greatest potentials in life.

He's the chairman of Kelly Benedict International (KBI), a personal and professional development company. KBI programs are designed to motivate the minds of audience, challenge their thoughts, empower them to think and take immediate action that will lead to extraordinary results.

He is also the founder of Kelly Benedict Child Support Initiatives (KBCSI), a global initiative that aims at providing books, tools and workshops for positive parenting as well as helping high school students attain their academic goals, realize their dreams, live a fulfilled life and become a responsible citizen.

His new series *Promoting Student Success* is geared towards strengthening teachers-student relationship, helping parents raise well-balanced children, and sharing values that improve students' academics and prepare them for life.

Kelly earned his degree from Coventry University, United Kingdom. He currently resides in Abuja.

Books by Kelly Benedict

- Promoting Student Success: What Are My Roles As A Parent

- Promoting Student Success: Power Keys To Achieving Academic Excellence

- Focusing Change To Win: Leadership Change Manual

Kelly Benedict International

For additional copies of this book and a complete list
of our titles, please visit us at:
Official website: www.kellybenedict.com
Child Initiative: www.kbcin.org
Email: book@kellybenedict.com
Mobile: +2348159994865 | +2348178848227